PARENT'S GUIDE TO THE OHIO PROFICIENCY TESTS FOR GRADE 4: READING, WRITING, AND MATHEMATICS

Cynthia and Drew Johnson

Simon & Schuster

NEW YORK · LONDON · SINGAPORE · SYDNEY · TORONTO

Kaplan Publishing
Published by Simon & Schuster
1230 Avenue of the Americas
New York, NY 10020

For bulk sales to schools, colleges, and universities, please contact: Order Department, Simon & Schuster, 100 Front Street, Riverside, NJ 08075. Phone: 1-800-223-2336. Fax: 1-800-943-9831

Project Editor: Megan Duffy
Contributing Editor: Marc Bernstein
Cover Design: Cheung Tai
Interior Page Design: Gumption Design
Production Editor: Maude Spekes
Desktop Publishing Manager: Michael Shevlin
Managing Editor: Dave Chipps
Executive Editor: Del Franz

Special thanks to: Rudy Robles

Manufactured in the United States of America

December 2000

10 9 8 7 6 5 4 3 2 1

ISBN 0-7432-0496-4

All of the practice questions in this book were created by the authors to illustrate question types. They are not actual test questions. For more information on the Ohio Proficiency Tests, including sample questions and answers and past results, visit the Ohio Department of Education's Web site at http://www.ode.state.oh.us.

CONTENTS

Acknowledgments

The authors would like to thank Maureen McMahon, Lori DeGeorge, and Megan Duffy for their enormous contributions towards making this book a reality.

INTRODUCTION

Although several years have passed since you were nine years old, your grade school experience is probably not very different from your child's. There are still spelling bees at school, dodgeball games at recess, and giggling fits during class in which students try to stop laughing, but just can't. These are all memories you can share with your child. However, the memory of spending time in intensive preparation for a series of standardized tests is one your child will have all on his own.

The tests in question are the Ohio Proficiency Tests, or the OPTs. The Proficiency exams for grade four, which roughly 130,000 children take annually, are similar to the OPTs given to all Ohio sixth-graders around the same time. Since its inception, the Grade 4 OPTs have consisted of five different tests on the following subjects: Writing, Reading, Mathematics, Citizenship, and Science. At the time of this book's publication, however, the future of the Citizenship and Science tests was up in the air. The governor and other state politicians, as well as parents themselves, were looking to scale back the OPTs in order to focus on the English Language Arts (Reading and Writing) and Math. *Parent's Guide to the Ohio Proficiency Tests for Grade 4* will do the same: concentrate on *Reading, Writing, and Mathematics* test subjects and strategies. But in the event that all five tests are kept intact, we have included a brief Citizenship and Science review chapter towards the back of this book.

> ## Testing *en Español*—and Other Special Cases
>
> The current criteria allows students with limited English proficiency to gain an exemption if they have had less than two years of English instruction. While this is a general rule, there are always exceptions, so parents should clarify their child's test-taking rights with their local school districts in order to prevent any sort of misunderstanding. This also holds true for parents of students with disabilities.

Except for the Writing test, each of these exams is a combination of multiple-choice, short-answer, and extended-response questions; the writing exam consists of two writing assignments. Critics of the tests could state that some IRS forms are easier to understand than this test format. While this might be true, if you and your child take the time to familiarize yourselves with the test structure, your child will not be confused or frustrated by the test format, and will instead approach the exam experience with the confidence of a veteran accountant handling a 1040EZ form.

How the OPTs Were Born

A little history will help put these tests in perspective. Ohio first started a mandatory testing program in 1987 for ninth-graders, and then expanded to other grades. The fourth-grade tests became mandatory in 1994.

How are these tests developed? The Ohio Department of Education assembles content review committees to decide upon the Learning Outcomes for grade 4—i.e, model courses of study in writing, reading, math, citizenship, and science. Originally, the Proficiency Tests were merely used to identify students who needed additional academic help, but this changed once the Ohio Senate Bill 55 took effect in 1998. As part of its "Fourth-Grade Guarantee," the bill requires fourth-graders who score below proficiency on the Reading OPT to attend summer school. Since the proficiency rate on the fourth-grade Reading exam is normally around 50 to 60 percent, a large number of fourth-graders have been enrolled in summer school. However, at the time of this book's publication, debate and controversy over this "Fourth-Grade Guarantee" bill may lead to its alteration or revocation.

Every Test Matters

While the Reading test is very important under current regulations, the other exams are also significant. A student who scores below standards in three or more of the tests will be offered summer remediation, and the district has the option of retaining the student as well.

While these tests are high stakes, there are some exceptions to the rule. If a student's teacher and principal both agree that the child is ready for the fifth grade, a failing Reading score is overruled. Also, students with disabilities can be advanced to the next grade if their Individual Education Plan excuses them from taking the tests.

How You Can Help

Many of you are already aware of how important the Proficiency Tests are to your child, which is why you picked up this book in the first place. While your child's teacher is probably already doing some exam-related work in the classroom, nothing is better for your child than receiving personal tutoring from someone she trusts. Since Mr. Rogers is very busy this time of year, that person will have to be you. Contained inside this book are all the facts, tips, questions, activities, and advice you will need to help your child succeed on the OPTs. *Parent's Guide to the Ohio Proficiency Tests for Grade 4: Reading, Writing, and Mathematics* lets you know exactly what skills are being tested on these exams, gives you test-taking strategies to make approaching these tests easier, and tells you exactly how to teach your child these skills and strategies. By analyzing and discussing the tests in detail, our goal is not only to provide you and your child with the basic knowledge she needs to excel on the tests, but also to instill a sense of confidence through familiarity, since feeling confident and prepared for these long, involved exams is a key factor in how a student fares on the tests.

After reading this book, both you and your child should feel ready to take on the tests first—and then the fifth grade. While that feeling might not do you any good in your adult life, it will do wonders for your kid.

Chapter One THE A's, B's, C's, AND D's OF GOOD TEST TAKING

Does the mere sight of a No. 2 pencil cause your child to break into a cold, trembling sweat? Are the words *multiple-choice* or *essay* invariably followed by a thin, keening shriek or forlorn wail? If the answer to either of these questions is "yes," then it's time you faced the facts: When it comes to taking standardized tests, your child is just like everyone else.

The vast majority of Americans experience some fear and nervousness before taking a big test. It is only natural that a nine-year-old would feel anxious when faced with a test that might cause him to have to take summer school, or maybe even be held back a grade. Sure, there are a few folks out there who are perfectly calm when faced with exams, but they are all either hopelessly insane or currently making a living writing test-preparation materials.

Let your kid know that it is normal to be nervous about the unknown, but that the more he knows about the

The Breakdown

Students have two and a half hours for each test, although each test is designed to be completed within 75 minutes. All multiple-choice questions have three possible answer choices (only one of which is correct) and are worth one point each. Short-answer questions are worth two points apiece, while extended-response problems are worth four points each. These distributions do not include the embedded field-test items (see page 10).

Writing OPT:

During this test students will be given a short amount of text to read, followed by two writing assignments. Each assignment will be given a score from 0–4 points.

Reading OPT:

4–6 reading passages, followed by 38 questions total: 30 multiple-choice questions, 6 short-answer questions, and 2 extended-response questions.

Mathematics OPT:

30 multiple-choice questions, 8 short-answer questions, and 2 extended-response questions.

Citizenship OPT:

30 multiple-choice questions, 8 short-answer questions, and 2 extended-response questions.

Science OPT:

30 multiple-choice questions, 8 short-answer questions, and 2 extended-response questions.

OPTs, the less nervous he will feel. All the information and all the techniques we will cover in this book will ease your child's nervousness and replace it with confidence by making that "unknown"—in this case, the exams—familiar and manageable. Test anxiety almost invariably leads to a lower test score, so it is important that you work to boost your child's confidence about the exams. Just understanding the basic format of these exams can be empowering, as the OPT in Mathematics changes from a scary hurdle that must be jumped to simply "a 2 hour, 30 minute math test with 30 multiple-choice questions worth a point apiece, interspersed with six short-answer (0–2 points each) and two extended-response questions (0–4 points each)."

Learning about question types and little details, like knowing how many Measurement questions will appear on the Math OPT, serves a dual purpose for the tests: It provides your child with useful information, and it takes away the fear-of-the-unknown aspect of the exam. This principle is the foundation of successful test preparation:

Familiarity leads to confidence.

Think of the OPTs as that haunted house on the end of your street. At first, your child only knows the horror stories about the children who went inside never to be seen again. Your job as a parent is to guide your child through the exams during the day, showing how the scary noise coming from upstairs is caused by a rusty blind, and that beyond the usual dangers associated with an old house (loose floorboards, a rickety staircase), there is nothing about the place to worry about. If you can replace the anxiety and stress your child feels about the OPTs with a feeling of confidence, you will have done him a great service.

THE END-OF-SENTENCE GAME

For a fun way to quiz your child about basic OPT facts, try playing this game. For one evening (or longer), try to sneak in simple questions at the end of ordinary sentences, so that "Please pass the potatoes" becomes "Please pass the potatoes if you how many questions there are in the Citizenship exam." Your child has to answer as quickly as possible, and correctly as well. The game can be one-player, with your child working to get as many right in a row as possible, or it can be two-player, so that your child can say, "Dear parental unit, would you please read me a bedtime story and tell me how many different reading passages are in the Reading OPT?"

Why Cosmas Ndeti, Former Boston Marathon Winner, Would Probably Do Well on the OPTs

Although Mr. Ndeti, a world-class marathon runner, probably has not had as much work with fractions as your child has recently, he is very skilled in one crucial test-taking area: *pacing*. Knowing that he's going to run 26 miles, Ndeti picks a nice, consistent speed at which to run, and keeps at that pace throughout the entire race. What he *doesn't* do, and what you should not allow your child to do, is spend too much time in any one area or run out of gas before the race is over.

Although the Ohio Proficiency Tests give students an ample amount of time—the test makers have designed each test to take about half the time allotted for it—that doesn't mean your child should spend four hours taking every session. At a certain point, taking too much time becomes as harmful as taking too little: frustration mounts, boredom and fatigue set in. Perseverance is a noble trait, but on a standardized test, spending half the time answering one multiple-choice question is tantamount to standardized-test suicide. Your child should stay focused on the task at hand and never get too flustered by any one question.

One or two small breaks during each test is fine if your child feels her brain is getting strained. Tell her to put the pencil down, stretch out her hands and arms, take some deep breaths, and then pick up the pencil and finish the test. If your child comes to a question she does not understand, tell her to think of this as a guideline:

> *Spend up to four minutes trying to figure out the question;*
> *then, using the techniques taught in this book, take an*
> *educated guess and move on.*

The Ohio Proficiency Tests do not require perfection. There are only two real scores: pass or fail. To pass, students simply need to get about two-thirds of the questions right, so it is never worth their while to spend 50 minutes on one question that's stumping them, only to be so mentally fatigued that they do poorly on the rest of the exam. Certainly, you don't want to encourage your child to do less than her best, but she must realize that no one question is so important that it is worth getting bogged down on and upset over. There are always some questions that just seem baffling. Throughout the rest of this book, we'll show you how to show your kid how to make good guesses, keep her cool, and stay on pace when faced with a stumper.

In addition to telling your child not to get stuck on one question, you can also encourage the "two-pass" approach to test taking. On the first pass through a test, your child should answer only those questions she can handle quickly and easily, skipping over any questions that leave her confused or require a lot of thought. Seeing a bunch of ovals filled in right away often gives students a quick boost of confidence. On the second pass, tell your child to go a little slower, use process of elimination (a technique we'll discuss in a moment) to cross out any incorrect choices, and then take a guess and move on. The two-pass system is very helpful on all of the Proficiency exams, since it allows your child to answer the easy multiple-choice questions before tackling the short-answer and extended-response questions.

This is not to say that your child should concentrate on the one-point questions while blowing off the 0–4 point questions. The point is that the open-ended questions are harder and definitely more involved, and you do not want your child getting sucked into one of those to the

Book Talk

Unless otherwise noted, "open-ended questions" is the term used throughout this book to describe both the short-answer and the extended-response questions.

detriment of the rest of the exam. By saving them for last, your child can answer all the multiple-choice items, mentally ratchet her brain into open-ended question territory (meaning she understands that these questions will be more involved and take more time than the multiple-choice questions), and then tackle them.

This point is very important for the Reading OPT. After reading a passage, your child should answer all the multiple-choice questions about the passage first, and then work on the open-ended questions. This shouldn't be too hard to do, since the open-ended question is quite often the final one on each passage. Still, it is important for your child to realize these two question types primarily test two different skills. The multiple-choice Reading questions predominantly test your child's reading comprehension level, while the open-ended questions are more like mini-essays that analyze your child's writing ability. Your child should focus on one skill (and one question type), and then switch to the other skill, not jump back and forth between the two.

To help illustrate the importance of pacing, here's a little "test-prep fable" you might share with your child:

KAPLAN'S TEST-PREP FABLES: THE TALE OF ISHMAEL THE SNAIL

Call him Ishmael the snail. When all the fish signed up for the annual aquarium obstacle-course race, no one gave him much of a chance, but Ishmael was confident of his abilities. The starting gun sounded, and all the contestants took off. The goldfish Ahab took the lead, but he got caught up on a whale of an obstacle early on. He couldn't figure out how to get around it, and he never finished the race. The two Ya-Ya loaches were also very fast, but they made too many mistakes. They kept swimming under the hurdles instead of over them, and they skipped some obstacles completely, so they wound up being disqualified. The gourami started out at a good clip, but he fell fast asleep around the plastic plant and Ishmael passed him up. Ishmael ran the entire course at a steady, constant pace, rarely making mistakes, and when the final results were tallied, Ishmael was the winner. As his reward, Ishmael was named king of the aquarium. He now lives in a plastic castle and rules the other fish wisely and fairly.

The Moral: A steady pace wins the race.

Edgar Allan P.O.E. for the OPTs

One of the biggest advantages to taking a multiple-choice test is that you don't always have to know the correct answer choice. Think about it: The answer is already there, staring you in the face. If you find all the incorrect answer choices and eliminate them, you will get the question right just the same. The *process of elimination* technique, known as P.O.E. in test taker's lingo, is one that good test takers use instinctively, but that anyone can learn to do with practice. It is especially helpful on the OPTs because there is no guessing penalty. You see, on some standardized tests, a fraction of a point is deducted from a student's final score for every question answered incorrectly. This is known as a *guessing penalty*, and it is meant to discourage random guessing. On the OPTs, no points are deducted. A wrong answer simply results in zero credit, not negative credit, so your child has nothing to lose and everything to gain by making good guesses on questions he is having trouble answering. And P.O.E. is the key to good guessing.

To demonstrate the effectiveness of this technique, see if your child can answer the following question.

1. How old are the authors of this book?
   A. 4 years old
   B. 29 years old
   C. 35 years old

If this weren't a multiple-choice question, your child would have little to no chance of getting the question right. However, as it stands, he should have narrowed down the choices to either B or C, giving him a fifty-fifty shot of guessing correctly. Since, as we mentioned, there is no penalty for guessing, he should then pick either B or C and move on to the next question.

Use Process of Elimination to cross out incorrect answer choices.

Perhaps the hardest part about using P.O.E. is knowing when to use it. In the above question, for example, how would you know that A was incorrect? You could say you used common sense, and that would be a valid answer. In many ways common sense translates to a basic understanding of what the question is asking, and therefore what the possible answers could be. Ask your child the question below, and help him use common sense to get a general idea of what the answer will be.

Thomas had $4.00, but he gave half of his money away to his friend Jeremy for a plastic bucket. Then Thomas gave away half of his remaining money to buy some gum. How much money does Thomas now have?

Before looking at the answer choices, ask your child the following questions:

Could Thomas now have more than $4.00?

Could Thomas have no money at all?

Could Thomas have $2.00?

The answer to all these questions is *no*. The last question is probably the toughest. But even if that question is confusing to your child, he could still look at the answer choices and eliminate some incorrect responses.

A. $4.00

B. $2.00

C. $1.00

Why would answer choice A even be offered? Test designers put it there to catch the careless student. They know many students often glance at a question, feel unsure of how to work the problem, and just pick a number from the question that appears in the answer choices. Using the process of elimination—and thinking about what the question is really asking—can help your child avoid these mistakes.

Your child can also apply P.O.E. in the Reading OPT. The incorrect choices are generated the same way they are in the above question: Words are taken from the reading passage and placed out of context as an answer choice. Students who remember seeing the words in the passage mistakenly pick them as an answer choice, never questioning whether the answer makes sense. Here's an adaptation of a recent Reading question:

2.   Where did Farmer Ike keep his cows?
    A.   in the barn
    B.   at a fruit stand
    C.   in his house

Which of these choices can be eliminated? We hope your child will recognize B and C as unlikely correct answers. B is wrong because stacking cows into pyramids is much harder than stacking apples and oranges, and C is unlikely because no farmer likes to have dinner interrupted by a stampede crashing through the kitchen. Still, these were actual answer choices, because the words *fruit stand* and *house* appeared in the reading passage.

So far, all of the examples of P.O.E. have dealt with the multiple-choice questions, which comprise just over half of most of the Proficiency exams. While P.O.E. is not the best tool to use when writing an essay, it is a technique that can be used for some open-ended questions. Although these question types are not as amenable to P.O.E. as the multiple-choice items, many problems on the OPTs are multistep questions requiring the student to do more than one piece of work. On questions such as these, P.O.E. is an excellent tool to either find the correct answer or at least do work that deserves partial credit. For example:

Michael reached into his desk and brought out these seven pens.

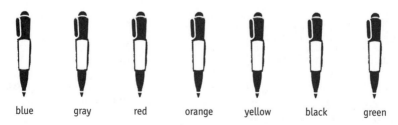

blue   gray   red   orange   yellow   black   green

Michael used one of the pens to color on a map. Use the following clues to find out which color Michael used.

Clues

It has fewer than six letters but more than
three letters in its name.

It is not the first or the last pen.

It is not next to the red pen.

What color pen did Michael use?

Explain the steps you used to find your answer.

In essence, this question is nothing but a three-step P.O.E. question, although instead of using common sense to eliminate answer choices, your child can use the clues given to him. With the first clue, he can eliminate red, orange, and yellow. The second clue knocks out blue and green, and the third clue eliminates gray, leaving only black. Even if your child messes up one of the clues and ends up with the wrong final answer, by describing which colors he eliminated and why, he could earn half credit on the question.

Have an Answer for Everything

Suppose your child comes to a multiple-choice math question that she can't figure out at all. She spends some time looking over the answer choices to see if there are any she feels she can cross out, but nothing comes to mind. Process of elimination fails her. Should she leave this question blank and move on to the next question? The answer is "No, no, no, no, no, a thousand times no!" Again, there is no guessing penalty on the OPTs, so every question must be filled in, even if it means random guessing instead of educated guessing (although educated guessing using P.O.E. is always better, of course). Advise your child to:

1. *Look for ways to work the problem using the appropriate skill. (On the open-ended questions, be sure to write down what skill is being applied, as discussion of the right technique could earn partial credit.)*

2. *Use P.O.E. to cross out incorrect answer choices.*

3. *Guess and move on, knowing that a test grade does not depend on every little question.*

If your child needs further convincing about the benefits of guessing, you might try telling the following story:

KAPLAN'S TEST-PREP FABLES: THE STORY OF KRONHORST THE FUZZY CHIHUAHUA BUNNY

Early in his life Kronhorst was just like all the other bunnies. He enjoyed carrots, frolicking in a pasture, and hopping up and down to his heart's content. One day, though, the Bunny Master came to all the bunnies in the world and said, "Okay, it's time you all got ears." (This happened a long time ago, when all bunnies were earless.) The bunnies had several choices to pick from: "long and floppy," "really long and floppy," and "tastefully long and floppy," just to name a few. Every bunny made a choice except Kronhorst, who couldn't pick between "cute and floppy" and "trippily floppy."

Not making a choice was the worst thing that ever happened to Kronhorst, because from that point on, everyone he met always mistook him for a fuzzy Chihuahua. "Look at that way too hairy Chihuahua!" people would cry, at which point Kronhorst would have to explain that he was a bunny. People would then ask, "But where are your ears?" Needless to say, Kronhorst got pretty tired of these conversations, as well as the endless invitations to the Hair Club's Annual Dog Show . . . although later in life he did make a lot of money investing in the stock market.

Moral: Answer every question on the exam or people will confuse you for a fuzzy Chihuahua.

While this advice is crucial for the multiple-choice sections, it is no less important on the essays and open-ended questions. There might be some open-ended questions that will look to your child as if they came directly from the Question Institute of Neptune. If so, tell her to write "Neptune" next to it, and come back later if there is time. However, she must not write "Neptune" more than once during any one session. On all other questions, your child should make her best attempt and be sure to document her attempt well. Who knows? Your child's guess on a Math OPT question might be the correct solution, or it might display enough sound math principles to garner partial credit. Remember, an educated guess has a better chance of being correct than no answer at all.

The Only Way to Avoid Mental Mistakes

There is nothing gained by your child's trying to solve any of these problems in his head. While it is impressive if your child can multiply big numbers without using pencil and paper, or work out scientific experiments in his head, it's not required for the Ohio Proficiency Tests. In fact, it even works against his score. Get your child into the habit of writing down all his work on problems and jotting down the main idea of a reading passage as he goes through it. Kids can eliminate a slew of careless errors simply by writing down their work. For many children, writing things down helps them clarify the material. Writing down work during practice sessions also makes for a better learning experience: If your child misses a question, at least you can go back together and see what the problem was.

Write down all work whenever possible.

As stated throughout this chapter, writing down all work is crucial on the open-ended questions. To illustrate this, read the following math example and then see how Imperious Student A and Well-Behaved Student B responded.

> Jonathan had $5.00 at the start of the day. At noon, he gave half of his money to Gwendolyn, and at 3:00 P.M. he lost $0.50 in a vending machine.
>
> How much money did Jonathan have at the end of the day? Explain your answer.

Imperious Student A: "Jonathan had two bucks *because I say he did. Now all must bow to the brilliance of Student A!*"

Well-Behaved Student B: "Starting out with five dollars, Jonathan gave half, or $2.50 away, so he had only three dollars left. Then he lost 50 cents, so $3.00 − $0.50 = $2.50."

The Number One and Only Child in the Class

Students are naturally leery of answering a question they do not feel they know the answer to, and they prefer to say nothing unless they are absolutely sure they are right. Teachers see this all the time in classrooms: Children refuse to raise their hands and answer questions because they are afraid of being embarrassed by a wrong answer. Unfortunately, this habit will hurt your child's test score. So explain to your child that on these exams, she should act as if she were the only student in her favorite teacher's class, and if she does not answer, the teacher will just stand there until she does.

Not only is Student A a megalomaniac, but he is also no better than Student B on this question. Student A provided the right answer with an inadequate solution, earning A only partial credit. Student B has the wrong answer but the right explanation, so B gets partial credit as well. Considering that about half of a student's OPT score is tied to open-ended questions, garnering a few points by properly showing his work could significantly boost your child's final score.

Although the example above is math-related, this technique is just as helpful on the Reading test as it is on the Math test. For the reading passages, have your child take whatever notes he is comfortable with, ranging from writing down the main idea to summarizing each paragraph. You don't want your child to spend a lot of time looking for the perfect phrase to describe the reading selection, but writing any thoughts he has about the passage will help your child understand it better. Since many reading questions test just how well your child understands the action in the reading paragraph, anything your child jots down to aid his reading comprehension should lead to an improved score.

The Field-Test Items

"Field-test items" are the name the Ohio Department of Education (ODE) has given to all questions on the OPTs that do not count towards a student's grade. There are usually five such questions embedded in each OPT subject test (except the Writing exam, which has none). Field-test questions let the ODE experiment with problems that could appear on future tests. So on one hand, the field-test items are helpful to future test takers because they allow the ODE to determine if the new questions are too hard or too easy. But on the other hand, your child will have to take the time to answer five questions that have no bearing on her test score. The presence of these questions just reinforces that it is never wise to get hung up on any one question: Your child might be exerting all her brainpower to solve a question that doesn't even count towards her score. Remind your child never to get flustered by any question.

"'Twas the Night Before the Test . . . "

Make sure your child feels confident and well rested on the days of the tests. Hopefully, this means keeping the nightly routine as regular as possible. You might want to schedule some sort of activity for the nights during the tests, but it should *not* be cramming. Trying to jam in tons of information before a test session is not conducive to a child's test-taking confidence, and it should be avoided.

A positive attitude is more important than any one fact.

If your child does want to review for a while, stick to the basics, asking questions about the test format and general test-taking strategies. These will come in handier than reviewing any particular parts of the different tests. Also, your child will probably answer most of the general test format questions correctly, which will boost his confidence. What you do not want is to have your child stumped by a series of questions, because then he will go into the exam the next day thinking he is going to do badly.

Here's a handy list of pointers for the time before the exam:

THINGS TO DO BEFORE AND DURING THE EXAM

1. *Make sure your child gets an adequate amount of rest.*

2. *Give your child a healthy breakfast.*

3. *Let your child have any medication if and only if he takes that medication on a regular basis.*

4. *Participate in some activity at night that is fun for your child but not too taxing. (Watching a movie on the VCR or playing board games are two ideas.)*

5. *Give your child positive words of encouragement right before he goes to take the test.*

You get the main idea. Send your kid to school relaxed and positive, and don't do anything to upset his normal rhythm. Some things that would *definitely* upset his normal rhythm and as such should be avoided at all costs are included in the following list:

THINGS NOT TO DO BEFORE THE EXAM

1. *Send him to bed earlier than usual, because he will just lie in bed thinking about the test.*

2. *Let your child have any noncritical medication (such as over-the-counter cold or allergy medicine) that will cause drowsiness or muddled thinking.*

3. *Decide to unwind by watching the midnight tripleheader of* Nightmare on Elm Street I, II, *and* III.

4. *Decide that the morning of the test is the perfect time to explain to your child how big the national debt really is, and what that will mean to him.*

Review

The Main Points Your Child Should Know:

1. Understand the format of all the tests, and be comfortable with them.

2. Maintain a consistent pace throughout the test, and don't let any single question fluster you.

3. Use process of elimination whenever possible.

4. Answer every question.

5. Write down all work to avoid foolish mental mistakes.

6. Make sure you are relaxed and positive on test day.

Questions to Ask Your Child:

1. What's the moral of "Ishmael the Snail"? *A steady pace wins the race.*

2. Ask general questions about the test format until your child answers the queries easily. *How many multiple-choice questions on the Reading test? How many answer choices for every question?*

3. What does P.O.E. stand for? *Process of elimination.* Why would you want to use P.O.E.? *Because finding incorrect answers and crossing them out gives you a better chance of answering a question correctly.*

4. What's the moral of "Kronhorst the Fuzzy Chihuahua"? *Answer every question on the test or be mistaken for a Chihuahua with a hair problem.*

5. When you should solve questions in your head? *Never!*

6. Who will love you no matter how you do on these exams? *Your parents, of course!*

11

Chapter Two READING

Questions on the Fourth-Grade Proficiency Test in Reading follow a reading passage that is about 400 words on average, although it could be as long as 750 words in length. There are usually 2–3 nonfiction passages as well as 2–3 fiction/poetry passages. The number of questions per passage varies, but correlates to the passage length (the longer a passage is, the more questions that follow). Many of the reading passages are culled from existing sources, such as *Cricket* and *Jack and Jill* magazines, which contain amusing, educational, and generally positive stories. If you want to give your child more practice at reading material similar to what will appear on the OPT in Reading—thus lessening his fear of the unknown—then you should:

OPT Order

The exams are traditionally given in the following order: Writing, Reading, Mathematics, Citizenship, and finally, Science. However, beginning in July 2001 schools will begin to give the Reading OPT three times a year (fall, spring, and summer), since this will allow students multiple chances to pass this test and thereby fulfill the "Fourth-Grade Guarantee" (if it is still in effect). Since the Reading OPT has been given this additional significance, it is covered first in this book.

Go to a bookstore or library and start reading children's magazines with your child.

This will help on many levels. It will give your child more exposure to reading testlike passages, it should aid in his understanding of such passages (provided you help him with positive guidance), and it should improve your child's overall reading ability. And, as if that weren't enough, it's also quality time!

Difficult or foreign words in the reading passages have definitions in the place called the Word Bank. There are also pictures with some passages, and occasionally 1–2 questions are associated with them. With this in mind, tell your child to:

Look for a Word Bank and look at any pictures before reading a passage.

There usually isn't a Word Bank, but if there is, your child will need to be prepared to run across some unfamiliar words. Looking at the picture should help him understand the passage better, and as we shall soon see, understanding the main point of the passage is a useful skill to learn.

As for the problems, question type is variable, with multiple-choice questions interspersed with open-ended items. Every passage will have at least one short-answer or extended-response question. For most students, the multiple-choice questions are going to be the ones they feel the most comfortable working on, simply because reading a passage and then answering questions is probably something they have done before. Since answering the multiple-choice questions after reading each passage allows your child to work the easier problems first, this chapter will focus on the multiple-choice questions first before discussing the open-ended problems. In general, multiple-choice questions after a reading passage fall into four major categories:

> Word Meanings
>
> Supporting Ideas
>
> Summarization
>
> Generalizations and Inferences

What Counts

As stated in chapter one, there are 30 multiple-choice questions, six short-answer questions (2 points each), and two extended-response items (4 points each). A perfect score would then be 30 + (6 × 2) + (2 × 4) = 50. The raw score—how many of the 50 possible points a student earns—that's needed for a student to be considered "Proficient" varies slightly from year to year, but in general is around 41 points. Since 30 points can be earned with the multiple-choice questions, how your child does on the multiple-choice questions is more important than her performance on the open-ended questions, which are worth 20 points combined.

Before we can start discussing each category, we will need a reference passage, such as the sample reading passage that follows.

Dashiell Learns a Lesson

Dashiell was a happy young ant who was always looking for a way to do things better. Dashiell thought that doing things faster always meant doing things better.

It was summer, and Dashiell and the other ants were busy storing food for the winter. Dashiell would crawl to the nearby field, gather food, and bring the food back to the anthill. It took a long time just to make one trip. Then Dashiell would have to *trek* all the way back and start again.

Word Bank

trek: walk or travel a great distance

flutter: flapping

"Boing, boing" sounded through the meadow. Dashiell watched as Rebecca Rabbit hopped up next to him.

"Where are you going?" asked Dashiell.

"I'm hopping over to the lettuce patch to get some food," replied Rebecca, who hopped once and then was out of sight.

"Hopping seems better than crawling any day," thought Dashiell. He raised up his hind legs and tried jumping like Rebecca did, but soon fell over on his face. When he looked up he saw Aunt Dawn had walked up beside him.

"Rabbits are rabbits," said Aunt Dawn. "You are an ant." Then Aunt Dawn crawled away to gather more food.

Next, Dashiell saw Sylvester Snake pass nearby. "That looks like a good way to travel," he thought. Dashiell laid his body on the ground and tried to slither like the snake did. He twisted his body on the ground for some time, but never made any progress. He stopped once his stomach started to get sore. Aunt Dawn saw Dashiell on her way back to her anthill and said, "Snakes are snakes. You are an ant."

Dashiell walked through the meadow. He heard the *flutter* of wings above his head. Dashiell looked up to see Carol Crow flying around in the air above him.

"What are you doing?" asked Dashiell.

"I'm flying around in search of food," replied Carol Crow, who snatched a tasty grasshopper out of the air.

"Flying seems like the best idea yet," thought Dashiell. He climbed up a nearby rock until he reached the top. Then he jumped off while waving his legs. Dashiell fell to the ground on his face. "Yipes," he cried, rubbing his head. Dashiell looked up and saw Aunt Dawn standing beside him.

"Crows are crows. You are an ant." Aunt Dawn left to get more food and shook her head. "Will Dashiell ever figure it out?" she wondered.

The next morning Aunt Dawn awoke and saw Dashiell crawling to the anthill with a load of food. "I thought you were going to fly like Carol Crow," said Aunt Dawn.

Dashiell placed the piece of grain down and replied, "Crows are crows. I am an ant."

Aunt Dawn laughed. "I'm glad you learned that lesson, Dashiell. Put that piece of grain away, and then let's go get more food to store in our anthill for winter."

Dashiell Learned His Lesson: Now It's Your Child's Turn

While reading through this passage, your child should be thinking about finding the main idea. What is the whole story about? Having a main idea helps shape the entire story, giving it meaning, which hopefully should help your child in her understanding. However, while learning the main idea is important, *memorizing* it is not something your child needs to do. The passage is not going anywhere after your child reads it. It stays right there for easy reference. Teach your child to:

Read to understand, not to memorize.

Once your child understands the action of the story, it's time to start answering the questions. Children sometimes try to read the story and then answer the questions

LOOKING FOR MAIN IDEAS EVERYWHERE

If your child is unclear on what finding the main idea means, ask him simply to tell you a story about something that happened to him at school that day. Since almost every story should have a point, when your child finishes his story, ask him to name the most important thing about what he just said. Another way to phrase this is "If you had to retell the point of the story again in only one sentence, what would that sentence be?" The most important thing should be the main idea.

Looking at a newspaper and discussing how headlines capture the main idea of a news story is another way to talk about the main idea. You can then read the story and come up with your own headlines. One exception: Stay away from articles dealing with intricate, high-level finance, unless you want your child's head to explode. By the way, if your child likes headlines, you can always play "Night of the Headlines!" where one night everyone speaks only in catchy, single sentences, such as "Child Heads for Bathroom!" or "Argument over TV Remote Leads to Conflict, Then Grounding."

without looking back into the passage for help. If your child does this, events could get jumbled together, which will only lead to incorrect answer choices. Tell your child that the Reading test is just like an open-book test. The passage is there for her to refer to, so teach her to feel comfortable going back to the passage to help her answer questions correctly.

Word Meanings

While some of the difficult words in the passage will have explanations in the Word Bank, other words (or phrases) will have questions devoted to them, asking your child "What does _____ mean?" It is then up to your child to figure out the meaning of the word by looking at the context, or how the word is used in the passage. Reading or hearing words in context is actually a good way for children to learn new vocabulary. It should be stressed that these are supposed to be new words, so your child should not be bothered if the word is foreign to him.

To help your child sharpen his ability to understand words in context, have him focus on the meaning of the entire sentence in which the word appears. Remember, in a multiple-choice item the answer is already there, so your child just needs a pretty good idea of what the word might mean in order to tell which answer choice is correct. Sometimes the meaning of the unknown word can be gleaned from the sentence it is in, but if the meaning is not there, then either the sentence before or the sentence after will contain the necessary context clues. Your child should never have to look any further than that—this is a fourth-grade test, after all. As he looks over these sentences, have him circle any clue words that he feels help him understand the meaning of the word. In other words,

Read above and below the unknown word.

After he does this, he should be able to answer a question like this one:

1. In the story, Dashiell thinks it would be fun to slither like Sylvester Snake. What does *slither* mean?

   A. slide

   B. fly

   C. hop

Hopefully, your child chose answer choice A, "slide." As you can see, Word Meaning questions do not ask students to give the exact dictionary definition of *slither,* just to choose the word or phrase that is synonymous with its meaning. When you ask your kid which words led him to that answer, he should say the words "like the snake did" and the phrase "twisted his body on the ground."

If your child prefers, tell him to look over the questions before reading each passage, and see if there are any Word Meaning questions for that passage. If there are, your child should pay close attention to the unknown word in question when he reads the passage, in the hopes of understanding its meaning right away. This may help him feel more empowered about the test, but if it makes him lose track of the overall storyline, it's not worth doing. In that case, just have him read the entire story and then be prepared to go back to where the word is in the passage.

Let's try another question:

2. Dashiell raises up on his hind legs in the story. What does *hind* mean?

   A. rear

   B. above

   C. top

The sentence with the word *hind* in it contains clues like "raised up on" and "fell over on his face," which might be enough for your child to figure out that *hind* must mean "back" or "rear." However, the sentence before also contains a clue, since Dashiell is discussing "hopping," an activity that every creature on the planet, whatever it might be, usually does with its back limbs.

THE MACKINUTE GAME

A fun way to help your child learn about context is to play the Mackinute Game. Take turns with your child substituting the word *mackinute* into a regular sentence. The other player has to guess what the word *mackinute* means in that sentence. For instance, you might say, "I like my hamburgers with pickles, lettuce, tomato, and plenty of mackinute." If your child answers "ketchup" or "mustard" or some other likely answer, ask her to pick out the words that helped her figure out the definition of the word. Try to make the game as silly as possible. Good luck, and may the best person mackinute.

Supporting Ideas

Plainly speaking, "supporting ideas" questions test how well students have read and understood small pieces of the passage. These questions are not about the "main idea." They are about the little details that, combined, make up the whole of the passage. For example, say you told your child the following story:

A clown in a blue suit walks into a bank with a large duck on his head. The clown goes up to a teller, who asks, "Is it hard to keep that thing balanced like that?"

"Not really," replied the duck. "I've got sticky webbed feet."

The Supporting Ideas questions would be things like "What color suit was the clown wearing?" or "What size was the duck?" These questions ask your child small facts about the passage that she is not likely to remember. If she tries to approach this Reading test the way she takes most tests (i.e., by answering questions from memory to test her knowledge), these Supporting Ideas queries are going to trip her up. Therefore, when looking at the Reading test booklet, it is important for your child to keep in mind that:

The answers for all Supporting Ideas questions are waiting for you in the passage.

This is another way of saying be sure to look in the passage to answer Supporting Ideas questions. Your child need not trust her memory on the Reading exam. Remind her that this is an "open book" test, and using the passage is the best way to get these questions right. From memory, can either you or your child remember which animal Dashiell tries to be like first? Even if you think you can, it is smart to refer to the passage to answer this question:

3. Which is the first animal that Dashiell tries to be like?
   A. Carol Crow
   B. Aunt Dawn
   C. Rebecca Rabbit

Looking back into the passage, your child should be able to choose C or to eliminate A and B, leaving C to pick. Either way, it's the correct response.

Here is another question:

4. Which animal in the story says, "Snakes are snakes. You are an ant."?
   A. Carol Crow
   B. Aunt Dawn
   C. Sylvester Snake

If your child decides not to look back at the passage, she might carelessly pick C. And she would be wrong! A review of the passage would lead her to the correct response, B.

Knowing where to look takes some understanding of the passage, but with practice your child should get better at reading a passage for its main idea while keeping a general idea of what events occurred when. Then answering Supporting Ideas questions becomes simply a matter of heading to a particular paragraph, reviewing the information, and answering correctly.

Summarization

There will undoubtedly be multiple-choice questions that ask, "Hey, what's the big idea?" More specifically, these questions want to know, "Hey, what's the main idea of this particular story?" Your child can learn to recognize these questions fairly easily, as the majority of them are written using phrases like: "This story is mostly about ____," "What's the main idea of this story?" and "Which sentence best tells about this story?"

Recognizing what kind of question is being asked is very important, since the question type determines the strategies your child should use to answer it. In this case, knowing that a particular question is a Summarization question is vital, since it means that the answer is *not* stated specifically in the passage. Your child could reread the passage forever and still not find the answer. That's why you should explain that . . .

To answer the "mostly about" questions, get the Big Picture.

Your child will have to glean a general idea of what the reading passage is about, and then use process of elimination when reviewing the answer choices. Having a general idea of the meaning of the passage helps students separate the right answer from the wrong ones, which is another reason why working on finding the main idea with your child is such a useful activity. The wrong choices are often actual facts from the passage, so they can be very appealing options. But remind your child that just because a piece of information appears in the passage doesn't make it the *main* idea. A good way to think about it—and if your child can understand this, he's on his way to a successful career as a standardized test taker—is that wrong answers on Summarization questions are often the right answer on Supporting Ideas questions, and vice versa. Get it?

HOW WATCHING TV CAN HELP IMPROVE YOUR CHILD'S SCORE

Granted, there's a catch: It has to be educational television. But if your child enjoys watching nature shows, one way to practice Summarization is to ask her to summarize sections of these shows in her own words. Nature shows, on channels ranging from Discovery to PBS, are almost always broken down into segments like "Here's how the meercats defend their territory" or "Two rams fight to see who's the toughest ram in the herd" or "Here a pack of hyenas go to the automated teller machine to get some money for the baseball doubleheader." This game can be played with other shows, but nature shows are a good place to start. This is because nature segments often have a general point, yet one that is never stated outright by the narrator who is often spending all his time trying to sound majestic.

Have your child think about the Dashiell passage, and what the point of the story was, and then attempt the question below.

5. What is the main idea of this story?
    A. Dashiell learns to be himself.
    B. Dashiell likes to goof around.
    C. Dashiell wants to be like a crow.

Notice that C is an actual fact from one part of the story, but not the correct answer, which is A.

Let's try another question.

6. Which sentence best tells about this story?
    A. Dashiell tried other ways of moving but learned that the ant way works the best for him.
    B. A rabbit, a snake, and a crow all showed Dashiell how they move around the meadow.
    C. Dashiell carried food from the meadow to the anthill and back again.

While B and C are all factual, none of them encapsulates the main point of the story, which, again, is A.

Generalizations and Inferences

Inference questions, as you might expect, compel the student to infer an answer not stated specifically in the passage. Sometimes the question will have a phrase like *will most likely* in it, showing that the answer is not 100 percent definite, only very likely. Like Summarization questions, Inference questions force the student to understand the passage and make deductions from it. For example, after the passage:

Sheryl was sick, but her brother Tommy, who was in grade school, felt fine. Sheryl's three best friends in high school were Angela, Tammy, and Brenda. Brenda lived next door, while Angela and Tammy lived across town.

An Inference question would be:

Since Sheryl is sick, who will probably to take her homework to school for her?
    A. Tommy
    B. Angela
    C. Brenda

While this example may seem a little arbitrary (What if Tommy's grade school was next door to Sheryl's high school? What if Brenda went to a private school?), the question does contains the phrase *will probably,* which goes to show you that the ODE (Ohio Department of Education) knows the meaning of CYA.

From the Dashiell passage, an Inference question might look like:

7. Why does Aunt Dawn keep telling Dashiell "you are an ant"?
   A. Because she wants Dashiell to give up hope of ever improving himself.
   B. Because she wants Dashiell to be comfortable with what he is.
   C. Because she believes that Dashiell should help more with his chores.

Nowhere in the passage does it explicitly state Aunt Dawn's reason for constantly telling Dashiell, "You are an ant." It is up to your child to deduce from the passage that Aunt Dawn tells Dashiell this because she "wants Dashiell to be comfortable with what he is"—answer B.

Process of Elimination can also be used on the above question. It is important for your child to realize that these passages are written at the fourth-grade level, and when it comes to emotions:

Good feelings beat bad feelings most of the time.

The reading passages are not written by a bitter, impoverished author angry at the world, no matter what anyone else tells you. They are written by former educators, and because of this there are no depressing stories about gambling addiction or people fighting and dying in a senseless war. So if there is an Inference question that asks how a teacher feels, answer choices like "angry," "hateful," or "moronic" can always be crossed out, and if a question asks why an aunt is acting a certain way towards her nephew, surely the reasons are going to be positive ones. Aunt Dawn, then, is not going to believe choice A, which is negative, and C is borderline stern. The best answer choice is B, as it is just the sort of positive, character-building answer that former educators writing the test would want children to learn.

What Kind of Question is That?

Knowing the differences between the four question categories helps you figure out how to approach each question. To work with your child and help him distinguish all categories, discuss the difference between the Word Meanings and Supporting Ideas categories, which require specific information from the passage, and the Summarization and Inference categories, which ask your child to interpret information from the passage.

The Short-Answer Questions: Get Visual

For the most part, short-answer items are like multiple-choice questions without answer choices. They are often two-part questions, so it's fairly easy to see that each part of the question is worth one point. Let's revisit Question 3, a multiple-choice item from earlier in this chapter:

3. Which is the first animal that Dashiell tries to be like?

    A. Carol Crow

    B. Aunt Dawn

    C. Rebecca Rabbit

The short-answer version of this question would look like this:

8. Dashiell tries to act like several different animals.

    Which is the first animal that Dashiell tries to be like?

    _____

    Which is the second animal that Dashiell tries to be like?

    _____

Questions 3 and 8 are essentially the same, only the short-answer question is immune to P.O.E. since there are no answer choices to eliminate.

> ### *Like multiple-choice questions, short-answer questions can be answered by referring back to the passage to find the correct information.*

Sometimes the process of looking back into the passage takes longer on short-answer questions, since students are naturally more cautious when filling in a blank line than when they are picking a choice that's already there. This is one reason why short-answer questions should only be attempted after all the multiple-choice questions have been answered, as it allows your child to use the two-pass system and work all the simpler problems first.

In addition to having no answer choices present, short-answer questions often show up in some visual form, since the ODE wants a certain number of open-ended items to have a visual component. An example of this is the wheel-type graphic shown on the next page.

9. Dashiell tries to act like several different animals. In the ovals below fill in two animals that Dashiell tries to be like.

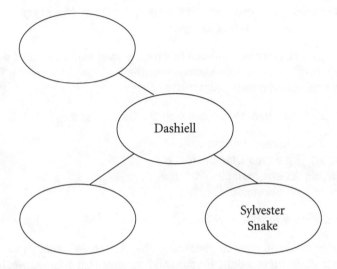

As you can see, the only difference between this short-answer question and the one before it is its appearance. But if your child didn't know a question like this was coming, she might get flustered by its strange appearance, and getting flustered doesn't do anyone's score any good. However, if you show your child this question and tell her that some of the open-ended questions will have a visual layout, when she comes to one of these questions, she will have been expecting it.

Remember, familiarity breeds confidence on standardized tests.

The Extended-Response Questions

The most critical distinction between multiple-choice/short-answer questions and extended-response questions is the one your child is least likely to notice, and that is what is being tested. Multiple-choice and short-answer questions test to see how well your child understands a passage, while the extended-response questions measure how well your child can write down his thoughts about what he has just read. All of the questions are still tied to the passage, but the added component of writing down an answer in one's own words makes it a whole different ballgame.

Make sure your child wears his writing cap, because putting down a lot of words is one of the keys to performing well on these questions. This is not to say that writing down just anything is effective, either—your child cannot filibuster his way to a higher score. Instead, being prepared to write down a lot is important, because being afraid to write *anything* is a certain recipe for disaster.

Extended-response questions often ask for an answer "in your own words," but your child must back up the answer with information derived from the passage. Therefore, he must remember:

If you can support your answer with examples from the story, then it is right.

Your child's answer might not be correct enough to earn the maximum number of points for that question, but if he uses the information from the passage in at least a fairly accurate manner, then he should garner at least partial credit.

Here are two sample extended-response questions on the Dashiell passage:

10. What might have happened to Dashiell if he continued to act like a rabbit for the rest of the year? Use details and examples from the story to explain your answer.

11. Retell Dashiell's story in your own words.

As for Question 10, your child will have to understand the passage well enough to make some deductions about it. In other words, if your child thought that Dashiell would do just fine emulating a rabbit for the rest of his life, he would not be in a position to gain any credit on this question. However, if he understands that acting like a rabbit for a long period of time is not going to help Dashiell at all, then he need only write that down and back it up with a fact or two from the story, such as "Since Dashiell cannot hop like a rabbit, it will be very tough for him to store any food for himself."

At first, your child may be resistant to the extended-response questions, since most children prefer to know exactly the right answer instead of just jotting down whatever thoughts they have. However, it is crucial to your child's success on these open-ended questions that he feel comfortable in putting down his thoughts on paper. If your child is not so thrilled about writing down his own thoughts, here's a story to boost his confidence.

KAPLAN'S TEST-PREP FABLES: THE PRINCESS WHO WANTED TWO BADGERS AND CEMENT BOOTS

Everyone agreed that Princess Lori was without doubt the most beautiful and difficult person in the entire kingdom. When the king asked whose hand she wanted in marriage, Lori replied she would take the first man who came through the front castle door wearing cement boots and carrying a badger in each hand. From anyone else, this statement would have been called ridiculous, but coming from Lori it was not even the fourth most difficult request she made that day.

Lured by her beauty, many suitors tried, but all failed. These men learned the hard way that knocking on a door or turning a handle when carrying a badger is an almost impossible task, especially if you have sensitive fingers. And these men were better than most, who got shin splints from wearing cement shoes and never even made it out of the construction area.

But one day Umbagog the Woodsman came to the castle. A fierce man, Umbagog was so tough he normally cut down trees just by staring at them until they fell over in fright. Umbagog showed up outside the castle wearing cement shoes with steel girder laces while holding two of the biggest, meanest badgers anyone had ever seen. He took one look at the door, and then slammed his head against it, shattering it in one blow. Umbagog then married Princess Lori, and they both lived happily ever after for reasons no one could ever quite explain.

Moral: In tough situations, don't be afraid to use your head.

Another general point your child must remember is that pacing continues to be important while answering extended-response questions. It is very easy to lose track of time when writing an essay. Students start worrying over exactly how to phrase something, and pretty soon the test is already half over, and they've only read one passage. Don't let this happen to your child. Tell him to:

Set a pace and watch your watch.

Of course, this means you will need to give your child a watch to wear (or make sure there is a clock in his classroom) and be certain sure he knows how to read it. Although proctors will sometimes call out the amount of time remaining, it is still up to your child to keep himself on pace. Refer to the chart on the next page for pacing suggestions:

Question	Time Spent
Reading the passage	5–7 minutes/passage
Multiple-choice questions	1–2 minutes/question
Short-answer questions	2–5 minutes
Extended-response questions	about 5–10 minutes, but no more than 15 minutes

Once again, though, the key is not to spend too much on any one question at the expense of the entire test.

Chapter Three WRITING

The Fourth-Grade Proficiency Test in Writing has the same time limit as the other Ohio tests (two and a half hours) and consists of reading passage followed by two writing assignments. The reason the phrase "writing assignment" is used instead of "essay" is simple: Chances are fair that your child won't actually write an essay, and if she does, it will only be one of the two writing assignments. According to the ODE, the possible writing assignments are:

A *summary* (summarizing the reading passage)

A *retelling* (restating the passage in the student's own words)

A *fictional narrative* (creating a story that is perhaps similar in theme to the reading passage)

A *personal experience narrative* (writing about an event that occurred to the student)

An *informative piece* (writing an nonfiction piece/report)

A *communication* (a wide category, this includes writing letters, invitations, thank-you notes, letters to the editor, directions, or a journal entry)

If you happen to say one of these phrases, like "letters to the editor," to your child, and she responds with that glassy, vacant stare that only children can really pull off, it would be in your best interest to show her an example of a letter to the editor before she takes the Writing OPT.

Make sure your child is familiar with all the different forms of writing that she might be asked to emulate.

You don't need to spend countless evenings drilling on the nuances of thank-you notes. Just make sure your child understands the basic idea behind each of the aforementioned writing categories.

Grading

The writing assignments are read by professional graders—often teachers or former teachers—who assign each essay a

Extra Rewards

To be awarded the Advanced Standards accolade, a student needs to score 7 out of 8 points. While this would be nice, there is nothing major—such as being allowed to skip the fifth grade entirely—associated with this rating.

grade from 4 (the highest) to 0 (not scorable). The highest score would be an 8, but in order to be considered Proficient in Writing your child needs to score at least a 5. Simple math shows that a score of 5 could be achieved by a 2 on one writing assignment (a so-so performance) and a 3 on the other (slightly better than average). In other words, while perfection is nice, your child needs to understand that doing a competent job on both assignments is the main goal to earn a passing score.

To assign these grades, the readers consider how well the student has applied the nine Learning Outcomes in Writing, which are grouped into the following strands:

Strand	General Description
Content	How well does the paper present its message using supporting ideas and examples?
Organization	Is there a coherent structure to the development of the essay, such as a beginning, middle, and end? Is there a conclusion?
Use of Language	Does the paper use correct words in the correct manner? For instance, are transitional devices used properly?
Writing Conventions	Does the paper have proper punctuation, spelling, capitalization, and variation in sentence structure?

In general, content is more important than grammar, so tell your child:

> ***When planning your writing assignment, concentrate on the content and don't worry as much about the grammar.***

Your child can always go through before time runs out and check over his spelling and grammar, correcting any mistakes that he may find. However, writing an unconvincing essay from the start will set him on the path to a lower score.

Stage 1: The Reading Passage

This passage is like the ones found in the Reading section. It could be nonfiction or fiction, and could be as long as 750 words. Since the Writing OPT passage is identical to the passages in the Reading OPT, the approach is the same:

> ***Read the passage to find the main idea and then be prepared to refer back to the passage if necessary.***

Here's a sample passage:

At the Plate

Jonathan was nervous. He had never worn his uniform before, and it felt uncomfortable. Jonathan stepped into the batter's box and raised his baseball bat.

The pitcher looked calm on the mound. He leaned back and fired the ball towards the catcher. The pitch was level with Jonathan's eyes. Panicking, he swung at the ball anyway. The bat swished through the air well below the ball.

"Strike one!" yelled the umpire.

His teammates starting yelling words of encouragement. Jonathan paused, then stepped back into the batter's box. The baseball came whistling through the air again. This time it was lower.

"Crack!"

Jonathan had closed his eyes when he swung. Now he opened them. He saw the ball sailing away into center field. He started running while the center fielder ran after the ball.

Jonathan reached second base and then stopped. He had made his first hit ever in a baseball game! And it was a double!

Stages 2 and 3: The Writing Prompt and Pre-Writing

Your child should read this story and try to anticipate what the possible writing prompts might be. To write a fictional narrative, students might be asked to finish the story. To write a personal narrative, the Writing OPT might say something like:

Like Jonathan, everyone has done something interesting
for the first time. Tell the story about a time when you
did something interesting for the first time.

With roughly 70 minutes to write each assignment, there is no need for your child to start wildly scribbling down the first idea that comes into her head. Rather, the key to the whole Writing OPT is in the first 10–15 minutes, when your child plans out her response, sketching out an outline of what she wants to say and what details she is going to use to back up her essay.

This sketching out, or Pre-Writing, is even encouraged by the ODE, as the Writing test itself will have a section in which your child can jot down notes. Occasionally, the ODE Pre-Writing section takes a strange graphical form, like the wheel-graphic on page 23, but don't let that fluster your child. Tell her that the Pre-Writing section is not graded, so if she wants to use the ODE Pre-Writing form, that's fine, but if she wants to write down her thoughts in another form, that's perfectly all right as well. Your child is in charge of the test, not the other way around.

The planning stage usually requires your child to write down details that will support her story. The more specific the details are, the better. Look at the sample first sentences next page. See how each one gets more specific, and therefore should lead to a clearer, better composition.

This is a story about how I built a car.

This is a story about how I built my first soapbox car.

This is a story about how I built my first soapbox car
with the help of my dad.

I remember clearly the day I built my first soapbox car
with my father's help: The morning was cold, chilly, as if
the night was still battling the sun for possession of the
Earth, fighting to keep its spectral, frosty hands
wrapped around our fragile planet.

These four examples could be graded Poor, Adequate, Good, and Very Good but a Little
Melodramatic. .

Stage 4: Writing

After thinking about and planning his essay, your child should spend 20–25 minutes
writing. Brief, clear sentences are fine. Your child needs to vary sentence structure a bit,
since graders are looking for that. But in general, short, simple sentences are preferable
to long, complex ones, because the longer a sentence is, the more likely it is to contain
a grammatical or punctuation error—which could cost your child points. Remind your
child that "stylistic brilliance" and "originality," though both components of excellent
writing, are not among the criteria graders will use when reading his essay. He doesn't
need to win a Pulitzer here. He just needs to stay focused on a specific topic and express
himself clearly and correctly.

Stage 5: Editing and Proofreading

After she finishes writing, your child should use any remaining time—and she will have
five or ten minutes if she stays on schedule—to check her work. One useful proofreading
technique is rereading the essay silently but aloud; that is, moving her lips as if she were
reading out loud, but not making any noise (since talking is not allowed). This slows
students' reading speed down a little and helps them pick up on errors they might
otherwise skim over.

Stage 6: Take a Break

Before starting the next writing assignment, make sure your child takes a quick break.
Get him to stand up and stretch, putting his arms up over his head. He'll probably need
to uncramp the fingers of his writing hand and massage it a little—there's more writing
coming up. He can take a moment and clear up any cobwebs in his head by forgetting
about the Writing OPT and thinking about something pleasant, like winning the lottery
or becoming the first person to receive the Nobel Peace prize ten years in a row. Now
your child is ready to repeat Stages 2, 3, 4, and 5 for the second assignment!

Chapter Four MATHEMATICS

Similar to its other OPT siblings, the Fourth-Grade Proficiency Test in Mathematics is a two and a half hour test consisting of multiple-choice, short-answer, and extended-response questions. The breakdown is as follows:

MATHEMATICS OPT

30 multiple-choice questions worth 1 point each

8 short-answer questions worth 0–2 points each (fill-in-the-blank questions)

2 extended-response questions worth 0–4 points each

5 field-test questions (do not count towards the final score)

Since this is a math exam, let's do some math and analyze the question-type breakdown. A perfect score on this test would total 54 points, with 30 points coming from the multiple-choice questions, 16 points (8 times 2) from the short-answer questions, and 8 points (2 times 4) from the extended-response questions. This means that the multiple-choice questions account for 55 percent of your child's grade, the short-answer questions account for 30 percent, and the extended-response questions—which most students spend a lot of time and mental energy on—account for only 15 percent of the total score. With this in mind, tell your child:

What's the Score?

Although the number varies slightly from year to year, 36 points out of 54 is about the minimum score needed to meet the Proficient standards on the Math OPT.

Take the time to answer all the multiple-choice questions first, then work on the short-answer questions, and use any time remaining to answer the extended-response problems.

If your child does not follow this advice, there are two major pitfalls she could fall into. She might set out to take the test from start to finish, but along the way get caught up working a long, difficult extended-response question which bogs her down and leaves her mentally fatigued. She blows her chance at correctly answering several less complicated multiple-choice questions, which are worth more points, by concentrating on that difficult extended-response item. She might also get in trouble if she rushes through the multiple-choice questions in order to have more time to answer the open-ended problems. This means your child has rushed through 55 percent of potential test points in order to work on tougher, more involved problems. Both of these scenarios lead your child towards a lower grade, and they should be avoided at all costs.

Here is another advantage of using a two-pass system on the Math OPT, answering all the multiple-choice questions first:

> *The fact that the multiple-choice questions count the most towards the final score is good news, because test-taking strategies are most effective on the multiple-choice format.*

What you want your child to understand is that more than half of all the math answers will be sitting in front of her, and all she has to do is pick out the correct answer or eliminate any incorrect answers, and then take a guess.

An Open-Ended Discussion about Open-Ended Questions

While the multiple-choice part of the exam is scored by a machine, the short-answer and extended-response questions are scored primarily by graders who have been given guidelines about what constitutes a four-point response, a three-point response, and so on. To get full credit, your child has to respond in a manner that is "complete and correct," meaning that not only is the correct answer visible, but there is also adequate work shown which demonstrates that your child arrived at the answer by using his math skills and not his powerful psychic ability.[1] If your child has the answer, but without any explanation, the response is not worth as much. So, as we stated in chapter one, remind your child that on every extended-response question:

> *Show your work, and give every question your best shot using sound math skills.*

The following little fable might help convince your child of the importance of this strategy:

---

[1]If your child does have such psychic abilities, tell him to concentrate his mental efforts on the multiple-choice section, since he doesn't have to show any work on those questions.

KAPLAN'S TEST-PREP FABLES: THADDEUS THE ARTIST AND THE 51 PERCENT FIRING SQUAD

One day in the kingdom of Schmooland, the king's loyal attendants were dusting the king's favorite painting of himself when they made an unwelcome discovery. Some villainous knave had painted a tacky mustache and ridiculous horns on the royal portrait! The whole kingdom went into an uproar, and the king demanded that all subjects search for the person responsible. Eventually, many Schmoolandians started to whisper that Thaddeus the Artist was the person who had made the unflattering additions to the painting. These people had no evidence, but were in fact jealous of Thaddeus and his hip, downtown lifestyle that included lots of coffee drinking, black turtlenecks, and incense.

In a rage, the king demanded justice, and although there was no real evidence, a judge declared Thaddeus guilty and ordered him executed.

"But judge," replied Thaddeus, "since there's no actual proof that I committed this crime, isn't it unfair to say that I'm 100 percent guilty? Isn't it more like I'm 51 percent guilty, and 49 percent innocent?" The judge pondered this statement, and realizing that his judgment was given only because the king was angry, decided that Thaddeus was indeed only 51 percent guilty.

The day of the execution arrived, and Thaddeus was placed before the firing squad. When asked if he had a final request, Thaddeus said, "Since I am only 51 percent guilty, I should only be 51 percent executed." The officer in charge of the firing squad agreed, and ordered his men to use only 51 percent of the usual gunpowder. When fired, the weakened bullets bounced off the artist's stiff smock, which was covered in dried paint and shellac. The officer in charge decided he had done his job, and let Thaddeus go.

A free man, Thaddeus then proceeded to find the real culprit, and then he wrote a screenplay about his exploits, which was made into a movie starring Harrison Ford that did tremendously well at the box office.

Moral #1: Partial credit can make a big difference.

Moral #2: Harrison Ford is a big-time box office draw.

All this talk about partial credit is not meant to encourage your child to not worry about getting the right answer. He should not answer the question, "What is 7 minus 2?" with the response, "Something around 3." The whole purpose of the discussion is to make sure your child does not freeze up when he encounters a difficult-looking extended-response question.

What the Math Test Tests

The Math OPT is designed to test Ohio students in the 25 Learning Outcomes in Mathematics, as developed by the Ohio Department of Education. These 25 outcomes are grouped into the following eight strands:

Patterns, Relations, and Functions (2–8 questions per test)
Understanding the rules guiding visual and mathematical patterns

Problem-Solving Strategies (2–9 questions)
Understanding the elements needed to correctly answer a question; determining whether a specific answer is in fact correct

Numbers and Number Relations (5–15 questions)
Basic math principles such as fractions, percents, decimals, order of operations, and comparisons

Geometry (3–9 questions)
Knowledge of geometric shapes, principles, and terminology

Algebra (2–8 questions)
Understanding the value of variables in the equation; looking at the keying sequence of a calculator and predicting the output

Measurement (3–11 questions)
Questions involving estimating and using units of measurement (metric and standard), as well as perimeter, area, volume, time, and temperature

Estimation and Mental Computation (2–8 questions)
Rounding numbers and estimating sums

Data Analysis and Probability (2–8 questions)
Understanding and creating charts and graphs; probability questions

The bulk of this chapter will cover these eight math strands in detail, but before we begin, we need to make one more point about the Grade 4 Math OPT. In general, vaguely worded questions in this section create a good deal of confusion for students. Questions in this section are rarely as straightforward as:

1. Divide 48 by 6.

Instead, the questions are often trying to see not if students can divide, but if they know *when* the right time to divide is. To accomplish this, Question 1 might appear as:

2. There are 48 people who need to be seated at 6 different tables. Each table must have the same number of people seated there.

   How many people will be seated at each table?

   _____

   Six more tables are added, and the people rearrange themselves so that an equal number of people are at each table. How many people are at each table now?

   _____

Or the same question might be seen as this:

3. There are 48 people who need to be seated at 6 different tables. Each table must have the same number of people seated there.

   How many people will be seated at each table?

   _____

   In the space below, draw a diagram to represent this information.

   If the restaurant found two more tables in the storeroom, and used them as well, how would this affect the number of people at each table?

   _____

   Two-thirds of all the guests leave by 10:00, and the remaining guests gather together. How many tables do the remaining guests need to use?

   _____

All three of these questions pose the same math problem, but to answer questions 2 and 3 correctly, the student must be able to say to herself, "Hey, this is a *division* question." (The third question, as you may have noticed, is an extended-response question.) This oblique approach to the key ideas is prevalent throughout the exam, which is why many intelligent kids get frustrated and wind up with a low score. They know a certain math skill quite well, but they don't realize that the test is often more interested in discerning if the students know when they're supposed to use that particular math skill. Once your child gets comfortable with the OPT approach, the math section gets a little easier.

Strand I: Patterns, Relations, and Functions

"Prepare for launch: 6, 5, 4, 3, 2 . . . "

What number comes next? If your child knows the answer to that question, he is on the path to tackling Patterns questions. Problems in this category can be either visual patterns or mathematical patterns, which involve sets of numbers. A simple pattern question may look like this:

4.   Study the pattern below.

What is the next shape in the pattern?

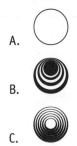

A.

B.

C.

On questions like these, tell your child to be prepared for patterns in groups of three or four, like the problem above. Why? While it would be rash to say that there will always be 3–4 shapes that repeat, consider what the test designers' thought process must have been. They probably thought a pattern involving groups of two would be too easy. Five is a remote possibility, but that would be very difficult, so three or four are the prime suspects every time. Since it is a four-character pattern in Question 4, the answer is A.

On questions involving repeating patterns, first look for patterns that repeat after every three or four characters.

Questions that ask the student to add up the parts that make up the pattern are a little tougher, and they often look like the following problem:

5.   This staircase is 4 steps high.

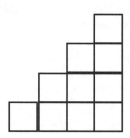

What would be the total number of squares if
the staircase were 6 steps high?

    A. 10

    B. 15

    C. 21

To solve this type of pattern problem, your child should *just continue the pattern and then add things up*. There are 10 squares to start with, so adding 5 squares and then 6 more would make 10 + 5 + 6 = 21 (C). Then it's off to the answer choices! Our old friend Process of Elimination could help if your child got stumped on this pattern question. Clearly, if we started with 10 squares and then added more steps, choice A could not be correct. Your child can cross out this choice and then take a guess.

Strand II: Problem-Solving Strategies

These questions are a little strange to look at, because they're not really about *finding* the right answer. They are more along the lines of, "Do you know *how* to find the correct answer?" or "Here's what the Binky the Random Student thinks is the correct answer; is he right?" Here are two examples:

6.   Phillippe woke up to go to school at 6:00 A.M. He left his house to walk to school at 7:20 A.M. To find out how long it took him to get to school, you need to know:

    A. When Phillippe came home from school

    B. How long he spent at breakfast

    C. When he arrived at school

7.   Jenna wants to place all her CDs into travel packs. She has 82 CDs. Each CD travel pack can hold up to 7 CDs. Jenna believes that if she buys 12 travel packs, she will be able to fill each of them up completely. Did Jenna solve this problem correctly?

    A. No, because 82 divided by 7 equals 13. Therefore, Jenna will need to buy 13 travel packs.

    B. No, because 82 divided by 7 equals 11 with a remainder of 5. Therefore, not every travel pack will be filled completely.

    C. Yes, because 82 divided by 7 equals 12.

In Question 6, the key is to realize that you need to know when Phillippe arrived at school in order to determine how long the journey took (choice C). The question itself is not so difficult, but most students approach each problem with the thought "I'm going to do some *math*!" But in this case, your child doesn't need to do any math, she just needs to determine what math needs to be done.

On Problem-Solving Strategies questions, the primary goal is to determine the correct math approach.

Question 7 does involve some actual math, but once again the real question is whether Jenna's approach to the problem was correct. In this case, it wasn't, as the answer is B.

If your child learns to recognize these types of problems, she can apply proper test strategy, which is to determine the best math approach. After that, these questions should be simple to crack.

Strand III: Numbers and Number Relations

These questions test a student's knowledge and understanding of such basic math principles as whole numbers, integers, even/odd numbers, decimals, fractions, ratios, and percents (you know, all the basics you learned as a child but have long since forgotten). What makes these concepts difficult is how they are presented on the test. Consider this question:

8. These four students are each wearing a T-shirt with a digit on it.

What is the greatest possible number the students could make?

_____

This is a question that covers up what it is asking fairly well. The trick is for your child to not get flustered if he does not understand what to do initially. He should ask himself, "What does this question want me to do with all these numbers?" After some calm thought, he will probably realize the answer is "Place the numbers in order from greatest to least." If your child is able to get over any initial weirdness associated with this question, he should arrive at 7,620 as his answer.

Make sure your child is comfortable with basic math terms.

Some of the more popular terms to know are *fractions, ratios,* and *percents.* Your child can be fairly certain there will be a question or two on each of these topics, so it is important that he truly understands and feels comfortable with these subjects.

Question 8 is a short-answer problem, in case you did not already figure that out. Here is an example of an extended-response Numbers and Number Relations problem:

9. Prakash and his father were playing a game in which one person would think of a number, and the other person would have to guess the number from certain clues. The first clue Prakash gave was, "I am thinking of a three-digit whole number that has the digits 2, 9, and 5."

List all the numbers that Prakash could be thinking of.

_____

Prakash's next clue was, "This number is also a multiple of 5."

List all the numbers that Prakash could be thinking of now.

_____

THE BRIBERY GAME

Numbers and Number Relations questions may also ask your child to read a word problem and decide what math operation needs to be applied. If you do not mind parting with small amounts of money, one way to simulate real-world math situations is to play the Bribery Game with your child. Assemble a collection of coins and then present various amounts of change to her and ask her how many cents she has. If she gets the amount correct, add or subtract various pieces of currency. Add or subtract in word form, though, asking your child questions like "If Bob has this amount of money, and Bob and Joanie together have $1.35, how much money does Joanie have?" You could also say, "If the amount of money here needed to be split three ways, how much would each person have?" If your child gets three answers in a row correct, she gets to "keep the change." If your child is very bright, stay away from using those gold dollar coins.

You can also expand the game to work on basic number concepts like fractions, percents, and ratios. For example, you might use a group of eight dimes and ask your child, "If I had 1/4 of these dimes, how many cents would I have?"

Prakash's last clue was, "When my number is rounded to the nearest hundred, it is 300."

What is Prakash's number?

_____

Write three clues for another number game and number your clues. The game must have only one correct answer. Write the answer.

_____

Quite a question, eh? All this for four points, which should show again why it's best to leave the extended-response questions for the end. Prakash's second clue, "This number is also a multiple of 5," basically asks your child to decide which of 259, 295, 529, 592, 925, and 952 can be divided by 5. Once again, it's a division question, of sorts, but it doesn't come right out and announce itself.

As for the final part of the question, your child would have to do a bit of work to gain that fourth and final point. Whether or not he cares to spend his time in this endeavor is entirely up to him, but the key point is: It should be done last.

Strand IV: Geometry

Geometry questions test students in several different categories.

Category	Example
Knowledge of different geometric shapes	How is a cylinder different from a cone?
Knowledge of geometric terms	What is symmetry? What is congruence?
Understanding of how an object will look if moved	What will Figure X look like if it it flipped upside down?

To tackle the first type of Geometry question, your child will need to:

Know all the basic two- and three-dimensional figures.

Two-Dimensional	Three-Dimensional
Triangle	Pyramid (with triangular or rectangular base)
Square	Cube
Circle	Sphere
Rectangle	Cylinder
	Cone

Knowing these figures is the critical first step to answering Geometry questions well. Knowing these definitions backward and forward is even better, as sometimes there will be an open-ended question that will ask your child to give a definition along with her answer. Here is an example:

10. Which of the figures shown below is a quadri-
    lateral? Draw a circle around any figure that is
    a quadrilateral.

Explain what makes a shape a quadrilateral. Write your answer on the lines below.

_____

_____

_____

This short-answer question is divided into two separate parts, and once again it illustrates how powerful partial credit can be. Even if your child makes a mistake and does not pick the correct figures (the third and fourth over from the left), she could still earn a point by answering the second part of the question correctly. Basically, anything along the lines of "a quadrilateral is a figure with four sides" should garner a point on this problem.

> ## SUGAR CUBE CASTLE
>
> For a time-intensive but fun way to teach your child about two- and three-dimensional shapes, buy a box or two of sugar cubes, get some glue, and construct a small castle using the cubes. All the basic shapes should be used: the towers could be cylinders, the front wall could be a rectangle composed of cubes, and pyramids and triangles could be placed along the tower wall. You may have to do some careful nibbling to make a sphere, but who doesn't like sugar?

In addition to shapes, Geometry questions ask about such geometric terms as *congruence, symmetry, similarity,* and *reflections.* Again, though, questions on the Math OPT will generally not be as straightforward as "What is the definition of congruency?" Instead, the question would give a figure, such as a rectangle, and then ask, "Which of the figures below is congruent to rectangle *ABCD*?" The student would then have to pick a congruent rectangle from among the answer choices. The correct answer will probably be "disguised" in some way, like being rotated 90 degrees.

A question dealing with rotation might look like this:

11. Which of the figures below shows the top figure after it has been flipped both vertically and horizontally?

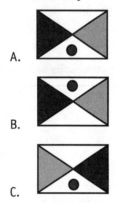

A.

B.

C.

Two basic test-taking techniques come into play on a question like this. First, there is P.O.E., allowing your child to at least eliminate figure C, since it is the original figure. The second important strategy is "show your work." Do not have your child doing these mental flips in her head—have her draw the figure flipped horizontally and have her flip the figure vertically. Artistic brilliance is not necessary, and neither is an ability to figure out this question in her head. Your child should just sketch out the two flips, which should not take too long. Even if it does take four minutes, four minutes spent getting a question right is better than spending three minutes getting a question wrong. The answer is B.

Strand V: Algebra

Normally, when people hear the word *Algebra*, they start thinking about words like "variables" and "equations." However, in terms of the Math OPT, the word best associated with Algebra is in fact "calculators," as many Algebra questions will look like this:

12. Look at this keying sequence on a calculator.

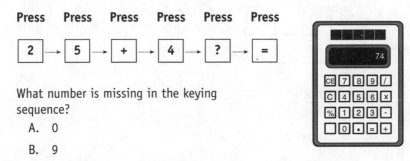

Press   Press   Press   Press   Press   Press

2 → 5 → + → 4 → ? → =

What number is missing in the keying sequence?

A. 0

B. 9

C. 29

This is a question that looks much more difficult than it really is, especially because of the way each digit is separated. To make things clearer, your child might want to rewrite the problem in a more conventional form.

```
   25
 +4 ?
 ────
   74
```

This question looks much simpler, but it's the same problem. Looking at the answer choices, C is obviously too big, and using 0 is incorrect because 25 + 40 = 65. The answer is therefore B.

So, the appearance of calculators signals an Algebra question, and rewriting the question in a simpler style is often the best strategy for these problems.

Strand VI: Measurement

Measurement questions on the OPT test your child's knowledge of such measurements as length, width, area, volume, time, temperature, and angles. In other words, does your child know how to find the perimeter as well as the area of a rectangle? Can he determine which questions ask him to find the perimeter, and which questions ask about area? The test booklet does not supply formulas for your child's reference, so he will need to be comfortable with all the various area, perimeter, and volume formulas for the most basic shapes before taking the test. He might encounter a question like this:

13. A group of construction workers stacked bricks in the following shape. Each brick measures 1 unit on each side. What is the volume in cubic units of this stack of bricks?

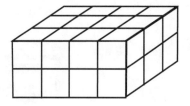

A.   8 cubic units

B.   12 cubic units

C.   24 cubic units

There are two solutions to this problem. The first requires your child to remember that volume = length × width × height, and so the numbers 2, 4, and 3 will need to be multiplied together to get 24. The other way would be for your child to look at the illustration and use common sense. Eight bricks are showing, but there are definitely more than eight, so choice A can be crossed out. At this point it is guessing time, or, your child could now put together 8 × 3 (since it is three rows deep) and get 24.

Another kind of Measurement problem centers around questions like, "Does your dog weigh 15 kilograms or 15 meters?" These Measurement problems test whether your child understands the basic units of measurement, and since no one uses metric units but everyone knows they should, you can expect that these questions will usually be phrased in metric terms. Here's an example:

14. Jimmy the Wonder Slug, shown below, was found recently on a South Pacific island. The picture below shows the actual size of the slug. Which of the answer choices best describes the length of the slug?

A.   5 kilometers

B.   5 millimeters

C.   5 centimeters

If your child picks A, then he has probably had nightmares of monstrous slugs destroying whole cities in their slime trail. The correct unit of measurement is C, centimeters.

Strand VII: Estimation and Mental Computation

Estimation questions are often easy to spot because either they have the word *estimate* in them, or they contain the words *about* or *round*. At this point, your child should turn off her internal calculator and replace it with her "I reckon" cap. Then she should:

Round off the numbers in the question, and then look at the answer choices.

Estimating questions are unusual, because normally math tests prefer a precise answer as opposed to a ballpark figure. However, estimating is a useful skill to have—especially since it helps your child answer questions like:

> ## New Term, Old Concept
>
> The ODE likes to use the term *front-end estimation* on some problems. This isn't some newfangled estimation that's just hit the market. Front-end estimation merely means that the student rounds off the numbers initially, instead of adding up all the numbers and then rounding off the final sum. Since this is what most people do anyway, the term *front-end estimation* is nothing to worry about.

15. The Fitzpatrick family drove 187 miles from Austin to Galveston. Then they drove 271 miles from Galveston to Dallas. *About* how many miles did they drive in all?

    A. 200 miles

    B. 400 miles

    C. 500 miles

If your child rounded 187 to 200, and 271 to 300, choice C becomes the only choice. And *I reckon* it's the right one.

Strand VIII: Data Analysis and Probability

The Data Analysis component consists of two types of questions involving graphs and charts: simple and advanced.

Simple = your child must read a graph or chart correctly

Advanced = your child must make a graph or chart correctly

As you might expect, the simple graph questions are usually multiple-choice/short-answer problems, while the advanced questions are the four-point extended-response questions. Simple graph problems may feature multiple questions referring to the same graph, and they look like the following:

The following graph shows how many raffle tickets Ms. Diaz's class sold during one week. Study the graph, then answer the questions that follow.

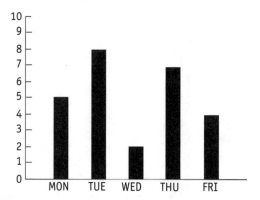

Ms. Diaz promised the class could work on their art project on the day the total number of tickets sold reached 16. The bar graph shows the number of tickets sold each day.

16. What day did Ms. Diaz let the class work on their art project?

    A. Friday

    B. Thursday

    C. Wednesday

17. How many days did the students sell more than 6 tickets?

    A. 2

    B. 3

    C. 4

In both questions, the test never just asks for information from the chart, like "How many tickets were sold on Tuesday?" In each case, your child needs to read the graph and then use the information in some manner. In the Question 16, this means adding up the ticket sales each day until the number 16 is reached, on Thursday (B). Question 17 is essentially a P.O.E. question: Which days can be eliminated because fewer than 6 tickets were sold? Only two days are left—answer A.

FOR THOSE OF YOU SCORING AT HOME . . .

Various kinds of charts are scattered throughout every newspaper, but if you want to go to the place that charts call home, turn to the scoreboard page of the sports section. There you will always find as many charts as there were games last night. Explain to your child what the various markings mean, and then ask questions like "Who had the most hits in this baseball game?" or "How many more runs did the Indians score in the fourth inning than the Yankees?" Questions like "This shortstop went hitless and yet still got paid $400,000 for the game. Where's the justice in that?" are socially relevant, but should not be asked to your child because they very rarely appear on the Math OPT.

An extended-response question might look like this:

18. Ms. Diaz's class sold raffle tickets for one week in order to pay for an upcoming class trip. The results are shown below.

Day	Tickets Sold
Monday	5
Tuesday	8
Wednesday	2
Thursday	7
Friday	4

On a grid, make a bar graph showing the number of raffle tickets sold each day. Use the information on the table above to help you.

Be sure to:

- title the graph
- label the axes
- graph all the data

Using the information from your graph, write two statements comparing ticket sales on the lines below.

(1) _____

(2) _____

At this point, no doubt many of you parents are feeling grateful that you do not have to take this test. Granted, this is a four-point question, and deservedly so, but it can still be completed if your child feels good about making charts. Any number of answers to the last part could be correct. Graders want your child to show that she can interpret the graph she just created. A correct answer could be statements like: "There are only two days where the students sold more than six tickets," and "The students reached 16 total tickets on Thursday."

In addition to charts and graphs, Data Analysis and Probability questions will have some questions dealing with the latter word, *Probability*. These questions can come in many different forms, so there is not really any one particular question setup your child should be on the lookout for. Luckily, there will probably not be very many of these questions on the exam. Don't spend too much time trying to explain the concept to your child. You may frustrate and worry her unnecessarily. If she is curious, you can try using a die to explain the general principle. Show her that there are six total sides on the die, each with a different number of dots. The probability that any side will appear when you roll the die is one in six. That's the basic idea. It is probably best to leave the discussion at that, unless you want to confuse yourself and your kid.

Whew! Believe it or not, that's all the math. It may seem like there is a lot for your child to remember. There is. But practice using the activities suggested in this chapter (and any others you can think of), and she will be up to speed in no time.

CHART YOUR VEGETABLES!

To give your child some experience making charts, you first need to buy some grid paper. Then, it's just a quick trip into your kitchen, where you can ask your child to graph all sorts of items. How many vegetables are there? How many different types of soups are there? Make sure that your child always puts numbers along the vertical line and a description of what is being graphed along the horizontal line. The rest is counting. If your child does a thorough job of graphing your food supplies, be sure to use the information on your next shopping trip. While everyone else has a shopping list, you will have a shopping grid.

Chapter Five CITIZENSHIP & SCIENCE

As we mentioned in the Introduction, at the time of this book's publication, the fate of the Citizenship and Science Proficiency Tests for Grade 4 is under debate in Ohio. In the event that your child is offered these tests, herewith is a brief review of the topics covered in the exams, and some test strategies you can work through with your child.

In terms of question-type breakdown, both the Citizenship test and the Science test are identical to the Math OPT, with 30 multiple-choice questions (worth 1 point each), 8 short-answer questions (worth 0–2 points each), 2 extended-response questions (worth 0–4 points each), and 5 field-test questions (which do not count towards the final score).

Many of the skills and tips covered in the previous chapters—such as the two-pass system, writing, reading charts and graphs, and our friend P.O.E.—are more than applicable to the Citizenship and Science tests. Having a good grasp of the basics of history and science is, of course, essential. But many students fall into the trap of overstudying, learning minutiae that won't appear on the test. You want your child to be knowledgeable about historical events and scientific phenomena, but excessive studying would just wear him out. This isn't a good choice, so concentrate on the basics.

Citizenship OPT

This exam is called the Citizenship OPT, but for all intents and purposes it is a history test. There are some civics and government questions, but the three key topics on the Fourth-Grade Proficiency Test in Citizenship are history, history, and location.

The ODE has identified 18 Learning Outcomes in Citizenship, which are grouped into these six strands:

American Heritage (5–11 questions per test)

People in Societies (5–8 questions)

World Interactions (5–11 questions)

Decision Making and Resources (5–11 questions)

Democratic Processes (5–8 questions)

Citizenship Rights and Responsibilities (5–8 questions)

What's the Score?

Although the number varies slightly from year to year, 42 points out of 54 is about the minimum score needed to meet the Proficient standards on the Citizenship OPT.

Strand I: American Heritage
In addition to asking questions about the history of Ohio and the United States, these questions often test whether a student understands the sequence of events in history. Because sequence is important, about 24 questions on each Citizenship OPT will feature a time line. Citizenship questions with time lines are a boon to your child, because often, these questions do not require your child to have any previous knowledge of a specific historical event, she just simply has to interpret the events that appear on the time line.

Strand II: People in Societies
A more accurate title for this content strand would be "People in *Ohio* Societies." This category focuses on the cultural groups that have lived or still live in Ohio, and while there are many different cultures, most questions in this category focus on one group: Native Americans. To best prepare for these questions, your child should learn the basic facts about how Native Americans lived before the arrival of European settlers.

Strand III: World Interactions
These questions are very easy to spot, since almost every World Interactions question comes with a map. Furthermore, the key to these questions is simply reading a map properly, so if you make sure your child is familiar with maps and map symbols, these items will practically fall off the map and into his lap.

Strand IV: Decision Making and Resources
Problems in this category involve such concepts as production, consumption, and what is needed to produce various goods and services. However, the most popular topic in this category generally raises the land/labor/capital question, so understanding the terms is the key factor here.

Land = things occurring in nature like trees soil

Labor = work done by people

Capital = objects like buildings, tools, machines, and cars

Strand V: Democratic Processes
To put it succinctly, these problems quiz students on the various branches of government, and what their function is. For example, a question might ask where one would have to go to renew a driver's license: the Ohio Supreme Court, Department of Transportation, or Lottery Commission? To get the Big Picture on Democratic Process problems, your child needs to be familiar the Big Three branches of state government: Executive (president or governor), Legislative (Senate and/or House of Representatives), and Judicial (the courts).

Strand VI: Citizenship Rights and Responsibilities
An intriguing content strand, Citizenship Rights and Responsibilities includes questions about fair play, the difference between fact and opinion, and working together as a community. To help your child, teach her to recognize that words like *most, best,* and *great* are all subjective terms which can not be proven. Therefore, when she sees these words, she'll know that answer is an opinion.

Science OPT

The Fourth-Grade Proficiency Test in Science is defined by 19 Learning Outcomes, which are identified from the four major skill areas, or strands, of the Ohio Science curriculum. According to the Ohio Department of Education, these four strands are:

Nature of Science (12–22 questions per test)

Physical Sciences (4–11 questions)

Earth and Space Sciences (4–11 questions)

Life Sciences (5–13 questions)

What's the Score?

Although the number varies slightly from year to year, 31 points out of 54 is about the minimum score needed to meet the Proficient standards on the Science OPT.

On the Science OPT, using your head can take you a long way, so make sure your child doesn't get flustered and think there is some high-falutin' science knowledge that he must have before the test in order to do well. Consider a question about shadows. Does your child need schooling in optics and parallax to know that the longest shadows occur when the sun is lowest, and that shadows are shortest when the sun is high? The authors of this book don't even know what parallax is, but we can answer a question like this one:

> A person is standing in an open field in Akron during the summer. Sunrise is at 6:43 A.M. that day, while sunset is at 8:52 P.M. At what time will this person's shadow be the longest?
>
> A. 7:42 A.M.
>
> B. 1:04 A.M.
>
> C. 1:04 P.M.

If your child thinks about this question, and uses common sense, he can find the right answer. Choice B is eliminated right away, because the sun will not be out, leaving only A and C. At 1:04 P.M., the sun should almost overhead, so it won't cast much of a shadow. That leaves us with A as the correct answer.

There are more questions involving common sense on the Science OPT than on other sections. While there is usually a precise, scientific explanation for many of the questions, simply understanding the basic scientific principles and applying common sense will often work just as well.

Many questions in the Science OPT contain a visual element, such as a chart or graph, in them. This is good news, because answering a chart/graph question on the Science OPT is the same as answering a chart/graph question on the Math OPT.

Strand I: Nature of Science

Along with the other Science content strands, Nature of Science is a broad category that covers a great amount of information. However, some key areas that occur with some frequency are: safety procedures, organization and classification of objects, and problems dealing with scientific experiments. The last category is perhaps the most important, as proper scientific experimentation is a process that encompasses many different fields of science. One thing your child should keep in mind: In order to set up any experiment properly—and answer experiment questions correctly—she has to understand the concept of a *control group,* a group that nothing is done to.

Strand II: Physical Sciences
Physical Sciences questions deal with the world around us. There are questions about chemical and physical changes; friction; energy; mass, force, and inertia; and simple machines like pulleys, levers, wedges, and inclined planes.

Strand III: Earth and Space Sciences
There is only one object your child needs to know in order to ace this section: the Earth. Earth Science questions talk about minerals, the composition of soil, volcanoes, fossils, erosion, and other things that make up our little blue planet. Still, it's important to keep in mind that your child doesn't need to be a volcanologist to know that lava is hot.

As with the other Science OPT categories, the key is in Earth and Space Sciences is to know the Big Picture about the topics. For instance, on a question about erosion, your child doesn't need to know high-level fluid dynamics; he just needs to understand that "water causes things to wear down, and so does exposure to wind." Students could spend a lot of hours in a library learning tons of different science facts, and while this would be good for their overall education, it's not crucial for the Science OPT. Remember:

> ### For the Science OPT, your child needs to understand the basic science facts, combine this with an equal ratio of common sense, and stir inside his mind.

On some science questions, good writing skills are almost as important as good scientific knowledge. Your child's skills as an essayist will be tested on some questions, showing how a technique learned in one OPT (how to write well) is often helpful on other OPTs.

Strand IV: Life Sciences
Life Sciences questions test students on how well they know the traits and habits of animals and plants. Does your child understand a basic food chain, with the little guys getting eaten by the big guys? If so, your child will do well in this section, or in corporate finance. Other Life Sciences problems ask about the difference between living and nonliving, and how animals and plants adapt to their environment.

This concludes our brief discussion of the Citizenship and Science curriculum frameworks. There will charts and maps throughout the both these Proficiency Tests—just tell your child to answer them the same way she would answer a Math chart question. There will also be times on the open-ended questions when your child's writing skills will come in handy. In other words, combining the techniques your child has learned in previous sections with some basic historical and scientific knowledge and a healthy dose of common sense will give her all the tools she needs to succeed on the Citizenship OPT and the Science OPT.

Chapter Six   I GOT A WHAT?!

Your child's scores on the Ohio Proficiency Tests will be broken down into three main categories: a raw score, a scaled score, and a percentage subscore.

The raw scores add up the total number of points your child scored on a particular subject test. So if your child answered all 30 multiple-choice Math questions correctly, received one point of credit on the eight short-answer questions, and didn't get any points at all for the two extended-response questions, his score would be $30 + 8 \times 1 + 0 = 38$ points. Since the raw score needed to meet the Proficient standards is usually around 36 points for Math, your child would pass that subject! Hurray!

Internet Information

For the most recent information about the OPTs, check out the Ohio Department of Education's Web site at http://www.ode.state.oh.us. This site has a variety of information about the Ohio Proficiency Tests.

Here is the breakdown of raw score and total score by subject:

Subject	Total Points	Minimum Proficient Raw Score
Writing	8	5
Reading	50	41
Mathematics	54	36
Citizenship	54	42
Science	54	31

The scaled score varies greatly from test to test, but the key numbers to remember are:

Subject	Minimum Proficient Scaled Score
Writing	--
Reading	217
Mathematics	218
Citizenship	218
Science	215

These are the minimum scaled scores needed for your child to meet the Proficient standards. The scaled score is derived from the raw score, but its range is much greater—on some tests it ranges from 26 to 419—and this allows school and districts to rate their performance with more accuracy. Therefore, while Student A and Student B might both be Proficient, Student B's scaled score of 260 beats Student A's score of 255, so technically Student B has mastered the curriculum better. However, this doesn't really concern you as a parent, as Proficient/Not Proficient is the biggest concern of your child.

In addition to these scores, your child will also receive a percentage score in the Reading, Math, and other content categories, which are the ones discussed at length throughout the various chapters: Numbers and Number Relations, American Heritage, and so forth.

Once again, however, as of press time, this is up for debate in the Ohio legislature. The scoring rubric may be altered such that the Reading score is broken down into four categories: advanced placement, passing, passing with remediation, and failure. This remains to be seen, so stay tuned to your state's announcements.

While a low score can be a cause for concern, it should not necessarily be considered an indication that your child is lagging far behind in his studies and that his education so far has been worthless. Be sure to discuss his scores with the person who is very knowledgeable about your child's ability as a student: his teacher. Your child's teacher will provide a better, more complete overview of your child's academic standing than a single numerical score from a standardized test. It is important that parents keep these scores in perspective. For instance, some parents might be disappointed if their child only meets the Proficient standards instead of the Advanced standards. But the fact of the matter is only 58 percent of all Ohio fourth-grade students met the Proficient standards on the 2000 Reading exam, and only 6 percent met the Advanced standards.

In terms of how the Ohio Proficiency Tests are scored, this is the end of the story. However, it should be noted that in this case, the phrase "end of story" only means "end of discussion on how your child scored on the standardized test." Your child has about a decade of schooling ahead of him. This test should be seen for what it is: an interesting checkpoint along a very long highway. Some students who scored at the lowest level on this test will go on to graduate from prestigious universities with advanced degrees, while other students who scored at the top will struggle to finish high school. Your child's scores simply highlight where he needs improvement. And the best person available to make sure your child receives that improvement is currently reading the last sentence of this book.

How Did We Do? Grade Us.

Thank you for choosing a Kaplan book. Your comments and suggestions are very useful to us. Please answer the following questions to assist us in our continued development of high-quality resources to meet your needs.

The title of the Kaplan book I read was: _____

My name is: _____

My address is: _____

_____

My e-mail address is: _____

What overall grade would you give this book?   Ⓐ Ⓑ Ⓒ Ⓓ Ⓕ

How relevant was the information to your goals?   Ⓐ Ⓑ Ⓒ Ⓓ Ⓕ

How comprehensive was the information in this book?   Ⓐ Ⓑ Ⓒ Ⓓ Ⓕ

How accurate was the information in this book?   Ⓐ Ⓑ Ⓒ Ⓓ Ⓕ

How easy was the book to use?   Ⓐ Ⓑ Ⓒ Ⓓ Ⓕ

How appealing was the book's design?   Ⓐ Ⓑ Ⓒ Ⓓ Ⓕ

What were the book's strong points? _____

How could this book be improved? _____

Is there anything that we left out that you wanted to know more about? _____

Would you recommend this book to others?   ☐ YES   ☐ NO

Other comments: _____

_____

_____

Do we have permission to quote you?   ☐ YES   ☐ NO

Thank you for your help.
Please tear out this page and mail it to:

Managing Editor
Kaplan, Inc.
888 Seventh Avenue
New York, NY 10106

Thanks!